Happiness in a Mug Cake

Happiness in a Mug Cake

**30 Microwave
Cakes to Make
in Minutes**

Kate Calder

Photography by Clare Winfield

Hardie Grant

B O O K S

Published in 2023 by Hardie Grant Books,
an imprint of Hardie Grant Publishing

Hardie Grant Books (London)
5th & 6th Floors
52–54 Southwark Street
London SE1 1UN

Hardie Grant Books (Melbourne)
Building 1, 658 Church Street
Richmond, Victoria 3121

hardiegrantbooks.com

British Library Cataloguing-in-Publication Data.
A catalogue record for this book is available
from the British Library.

Happiness in a Mug Cake
ISBN: 978-178488-654-7

10 9 8 7 6 5 4 3 2 1

Publishing Director: Kajal Mistry
Acting Publishing Director: Emma Hopkin
Commissioning Editor: Eve Marleau
Editor: Isabel Gonzalez-Prendergast
Copy Editor: Vicky Orchard
Proofread: Tara O'Sullivan
Design and Art Direction: Nikki Ellis
Photographer: Clare Winfield
Food Stylist: Kate Calder
Prop Stylist: Hannah Wilkinson
Production Controller: Martina Georgieva

Colour reproduction by p2d
Printed and bound in China by Leo Paper Products Ltd.

Contents

Introduction

Let's face it, there are few things greater in life than cake. But baking time and clean-up can be enough to put off all but the keenest of bakers. Have you ever had a cake craving but not been bothered to line a tin, weigh out ingredients, then to sit and wait for what seems like forever? Mug cakes are here to change all that. These delicious, single-serve miracles of science are ready to eat in minutes, and most of them are mixed, baked and eaten in a single mug. Less time making, more time eating.

Choose the recipe to suit your mood and treat your taste buds; these cakes are perfect for the whole family (minus the happy hour section!) but also a great quick fix just for yourself. The speed and simplicity mean you no longer need to wait for a birthday as an excuse. As well as being a great dessert, a mug cake makes a perfect mid-afternoon snack – and they're also great to make with the kids after school. In fact, they're so easy to whip up that kids can even take charge with minimal adult supervision. The speed makes kids feel included and engaged as they watch their creations come to life before their eyes.

If you fancy getting creative, you can top your cakes with your favourite icing or serve them with ice cream, custard or simply a dusting of sugar. Whether you're craving a classic vanilla sponge with sprinkles or a sophisticated amaretto and chocolate bake, there's a mug cake for everyone in this book.

Happiness starts here.

'Cake will always
be the answer.

The question is
irrelevant.'

Unknown

Equipment and tips

Minimal equipment is required for these bakes, and you'll probably have everything in your kitchen already. You just need:

- a microwave-safe mug

- a fork

- measuring spoons

- a microwave

And that's it!

The rise of each cake will vary. Watching through the glass of the microwave, you may be alarmed at the heights they can reach! They will have a big rise while cooking but then collapse like a soufflé once out of the microwave. Depending on the ingredients, some will shrink further, while others will stay risen just above the rim of the mug. Because of this variation, I make mine in a standard straight-edged 300 ml (10 fl oz/1¼ cup) mug, which accommodates all manner of bakes. But as you begin your mug cake journey, you will soon discover your own favourite mug: the one that suits the occasion and pairs best with your microwave.

Here are some simple tips for better bakes:

- The recipes are written for a 1,000W microwave. It may take a little trial and error, varying things by a few seconds here and there, until you find your microwave's sweet spot for timings.

- All the mixing for these cakes takes place in the mug itself. I use a fork to mix my batter. Like a mini whisk, it allows all the ingredients to come together quicker, avoiding any lumps.

- Once the flour has been added, just mix until you get a smooth batter. Overmixing can result in a rubbery cake.

- Accuracy of measurements is key. When I refer to 1 tablespoon, that means 1 level tablespoon. I will say heaped otherwise.

- To avoid overflowing spills, your mug should only ever be about half full of batter.

- Once baked, the top of your cake may look like it needs more time, but rest assured it will be cooked from the inside out. Overcook it and the cake will taste dry.

- The cakes are extremely hot when they come out of the microwave, so leave them to cool for a few minutes before eating! Especially if you're adding icing – you don't want it to slide off immediately!

- They do dry out quite quickly, however, so don't wait too long – these treats are best enjoyed soon after baking and should not be kept for later.

- If you are making multiple cakes, you must cook them in individual mugs one at a time in the microwave.

Chocoholics

Double chocolate chip

2 tablespoons caster (superfine) sugar

3 tablespoons plain (all-purpose) flour

1 tablespoon cocoa (unsweetened chocolate) powder

¼ teaspoon baking powder

1 medium egg

½ teaspoon vanilla extract

1 tablespoon milk of your choice

2 tablespoons sunflower oil

1 tablespoon milk chocolate chips, plus extra to decorate

1 tablespoon white chocolate chips or chunks, plus extra to decorate

In your mug, mix together the sugar, flour, cocoa and baking powder using a fork. Add the egg, vanilla extract, milk and oil, and mix until just smooth. Gently stir the chocolate chips into the top half of the batter.

Microwave for 1 minute 20 seconds, or until risen and springy to the touch. Sprinkle a few extra chocolate chips over the top and dig in.

Makes

1

Ready in

4

minutes

Salted caramel chocolate truffle

2 tablespoons caster (superfine) sugar

3 tablespoons plain (all-purpose) flour

1 tablespoon cocoa (unsweetened chocolate) powder, plus extra to decorate

¼ teaspoon baking powder

1 medium egg

½ teaspoon vanilla extract

1 tablespoon milk of your choice

2 tablespoons sunflower oil

2 salted caramel or butterscotch cocoa-dusted truffles

In your mug, mix together the sugar, flour, cocoa and baking powder using a fork. Add the egg, vanilla extract, milk and oil, and mix until just smooth. Put the truffles into the centre of the batter, one after another, so they are stacked on top of each another. The top half of the top truffle should be sticking out of the batter.

Microwave for 1 minute, or until risen and springy to the touch. Dust with cocoa powder and dig in.

Mocha

2 tablespoons soft light brown sugar

2 tablespoons plain (all-purpose) flour

1 tablespoon cocoa (unsweetened chocolate) powder

¼ teaspoon baking powder

1 medium egg

2 tablespoons sunflower oil

3 tablespoons espresso or double-strength coffee, cooled to room temperature

1 tablespoon chocolate chips

½ teaspoon icing (confectioner's) sugar

3 tablespoons double (heavy) cream

In your mug, mix together the sugar, flour, cocoa and baking powder using a fork. Add the egg, oil, and 2 tablespoons of the coffee, and mix until just smooth. Gently stir the chocolate chips into the top half of the batter.

Microwave for 1 minute 10 seconds, or until risen and springy to the touch. Set aside to cool for 10 minutes.

In a small bowl, combine the remaining 1 tablespoon of coffee with the icing sugar and the cream, and whisk until the cream forms soft peaks. Dollop a large spoonful of the coffee cream on to your cake and enjoy.

White chocolate and blueberry

2 tablespoons sunflower oil

3 tablespoons caster (superfine) sugar

1 medium egg

½ teaspoon vanilla extract

4 tablespoons self-raising (self-rising) flour

1 tablespoon white chocolate chips or chunks

1 heaped tablespoon blueberries, plus extra to decorate

icing (confectioner's) sugar, to decorate

In your mug, mix the oil, sugar, egg, and vanilla together using a fork until smooth. Add the flour and mix until just smooth. Gently stir the chocolate and blueberries into the top half of the batter.

Microwave for 1 minute 10 seconds, or until risen and springy to the touch. Top with a few blueberries, dust with icing sugar and dig in.

Mint chocolate

2 tablespoons caster (superfine) sugar

2 tablespoons plain (all-purpose) flour

1 tablespoon cocoa (unsweetened chocolate) powder

¼ teaspoon baking powder

1 medium egg

½ teaspoon vanilla extract

1 tablespoon milk of your choice

2 tablespoons sunflower oil

2 mint chocolate thins (I used After Eights)

sea salt, to decorate

In your mug, mix together the sugar, flour, cocoa and baking powder using a fork. Add the egg, vanilla extract, milk and oil, and mix until just smooth. Add one mint chocolate thin, lying flat on top of the batter.

Microwave for 1 minute, or until risen and springy to the touch. Remove from the microwave and add another mint chocolate thin on top. It will start to melt within seconds. Sprinkle with salt before diving in.

Banana, chocolate and hazelnut

2 tablespoons sunflower oil

3 tablespoons golden caster (superfine) sugar

1 medium egg

¼ teaspoon vanilla extract

½ very ripe banana, mashed

4 tablespoons tablespoons self-raising (self-rising) flour

¼ teaspoon baking powder

1 heaped teaspoon chocolate and hazelnut spread (I used Nutella), plus 1 teaspoon to decorate

In your mug, mash the banana well, then add the oil, sugar, egg and vanilla. Mix together using a fork until smooth, or as smooth as possible. Add the flour and baking powder and mix until there are no more white lumps. Add the chocolate and hazelnut spread and gently stir into the top half of the batter.

Microwave for 1 minute 20 seconds, or until risen and springy to the touch. Drizzle over a teaspoonful of chocolate and hazelnut spread, then dig in and enjoy.

The classics

Red velvet

3 tablespoons light brown sugar

3 tablespoons plain (all-purpose) flour

1 teaspoon cocoa (unsweetened chocolate) powder

¼ teaspoon bicarbonate of soda (baking soda)

¼ teaspoon baking powder

1 medium egg

½ teaspoon vanilla extract

1 tablespoon buttermilk

2 tablespoons sunflower oil

½ teaspoon red food colouring gel

3 tbsp ready-made cream cheese style icing

In your mug, mix together the brown sugar, flour, cocoa, bicarbonate of soda and baking powder using a fork. Add the egg, vanilla, buttermilk, oil and food colouring and mix until just smooth.

Microwave for 1 minute 10 seconds, or until risen and springy to the touch. Set aside to cool for about 10 minutes.

After about 10 minutes, either dollop or pipe on the cream cheese icing and dig in.

Tip:
To make your own icing, beat 1 tablespoon full-fat soft cheese with 3 tablespoons icing (confectioner's) sugar and a few drops of vanilla extract. It will keep in the fridge for a couple of days, perfect for your next mug cake.

Peanut butter and jam

1 tablespoon sunflower oil

3 tablespoons soft light brown sugar

1 medium egg

1 tablespoon milk of your choice

½ teaspoon vanilla extract

4 tablespoons self-raising (self-rising) flour

1 heaped tablespoon crunchy peanut butter

1 heaped tablespoon raspberry or strawberry jam

icing (confectioner's) sugar, to decorate

In your mug, mix together the oil, sugar, egg, milk and vanilla using a fork until smooth. Add the flour and mix until just smooth. Add the crunchy peanut butter and jam, and gently swirl into the top half of the batter.

Microwave for 1 minute 10 seconds, or until risen and springy to the touch. Dust with icing sugar and dig in.

Carrot cake

2 tablespoons sunflower oil

3 tablespoons soft light brown sugar

1 medium egg

1 tablespoon orange juice

½ teaspoon vanilla extract

½ carrot, peeled and grated

½ teaspoon ground cinnamon

¼ teaspoon mixed spice

4 tablespoons plain (all-purpose) flour

½ teaspoon baking powder

1 teaspoon raisins

1 tablespoon full-fat soft cheese (I used Philadelphia)

3 tablespoons icing (confectioner's) sugar

In your mug, mix together the oil, sugar, egg, orange juice, vanilla and carrot using a fork until fully combined. Add the cinnamon, flour, baking powder and raisins, and mix until just smooth.

Microwave for 1 minute 10 seconds, or until risen and springy to the touch. Set aside to cool for about 10 minutes.

In a small bowl, beat together the soft cheese and icing sugar. Alternatively use ready-made cream cheese style icing. Dollop a spoonful of icing on top of your mug cake and enjoy.

Use any leftover icing on your next mug cake; it will keep in the fridge for a couple of days. Alternatively keep spooning it on as you go. There's plenty of sponge to get through!

Ginger cake

2 tablespoons sunflower oil

3 tablespoons dark muscovado sugar

1 medium egg

1 tablespoon golden (light corn) syrup

½ tablespoon black treacle (molasses)

1 teaspoon ground ginger

½ teaspoon mixed spice

4 tablespoons self-raising (self-rising) flour

1 ball of stem ginger, chopped

1 teaspoon stem ginger syrup

In your mug, mix together the oil, sugar, egg, syrup and treacle using a fork until smooth. Add the ground ginger, mixed spice and flour, and mix until just smooth. Sprinkle over the chopped stem ginger, but do not stir it in.

Microwave for 1 minute 10 seconds, or until risen and springy to the touch. Drizzle over the stem ginger syrup and enjoy.

Rocky road

2 tablespoons sunflower oil

3 tablespoons soft light brown sugar

1 medium egg

½ teaspoon vanilla extract

3 tablespoons self-raising (self-rising) flour

1 tablespoon cocoa (unsweetened chocolate) powder

1 heaped tablespoon mini marshmallows

1 digestive biscuit (graham cracker), broken into small pieces

1 tablespoon pecan nuts, chopped

In your mug, mix together the oil, sugar, egg and vanilla using a fork. Add the flour and cocoa, and mix until just smooth. Finally, gently fold in the marshmallows, half of the biscuit crumbs and all the chopped nuts. Do not overmix.

Microwave for 1 minute 10 seconds, or until risen and springy to the touch. Sprinkle over the remaining biscuit crumbs and dig in.

Coconut and cherry

2 tablespoons sunflower oil

3 tablespoons caster (superfine) sugar

1 medium egg

½ teaspoon vanilla extract

2 tablespoons glacé (candied) cherries (about 6), rinsed, dried and halved

4 tablespoons self-raising (self-rising) flour

2 tablespoons desiccated (dried shredded) coconut

pinch of salt

icing (confectioner's) sugar and coconut chips, to decorate

In your mug, mix together the oil, sugar, egg and vanilla using a fork until smooth. In a small bowl, toss the cherries in the flour to coat them, then add to the mug along with the desiccated coconut and salt. Mix until just smooth.

Microwave for 1 minute 10 seconds, or until risen and springy to the touch. Dust with a little icing sugar and sprinkle on a few coconut chips, then enjoy.

Fruity

Apple crumble

2 tablespoons sunflower oil

3 tablespoons golden caster
(superfine) sugar

1 medium egg

4 tablespoons self-raising
(self-rising) flour

½ eating apple, peeled, cored
and chopped

custard, to serve

FOR THE CRUMBLE
2 tablespoons plain
(all-purpose) flour

1 tablespoon cold salted butter

2 teaspoons golden caster
(superfine) sugar

In your mug, mix together the oil, sugar and egg
using a fork until smooth. Add the flour and apple,
and mix until just smooth.

For the crumble, in a small bowl, rub the butter
and flour together using your fingers to make little
lumps, and then stir in the sugar. Spoon on top of
the cake batter.

Microwave for 1 minute 10 seconds, or until the cake
is risen and springy to the touch. The apples chunks
retain heat, so leave to cool for a few minutes, then
dig in and enjoy.

FRUITY

Pineapple right-side-up cake

2 tablespoons sunflower oil

3 tablespoons golden caster (superfine) sugar

1 medium egg

1 teaspoon vanilla extract

4 tablespoons self-raising (self-rising) flour

1 tinned pineapple ring, drained

1 glace (candied) cherry

1 teaspoon pineapple syrup from the tin

In your mug, mix together the oil, sugar, egg and vanilla using a fork until smooth. Add the flour and mix until just smooth.

Using a knife, make a cut in the pineapple ring so you can overlap it to make the ring fit your mug.

Microwave for 40 seconds, then place the pineapple and cherry on top and microwave for a further 30 seconds, or until risen and springy to the touch. Drizzle over the pineapple syrup, then dig in and enjoy.

FRUITY

Eton mess

2 tablespoons sunflower oil

3 tablespoons caster (superfine) sugar

1 medium egg

1 tablespoon double (heavy) cream

1 teaspoon vanilla extract

4 tablespoons self-raising (self-rising) flour

1 heaped tablespoon strawberry jam

1 ready-made meringue nest, roughly crushed

double (heavy) cream and strawberries, to decorate

In your mug, mix together the oil, sugar, egg, cream and vanilla using a fork until smooth. Add the flour, and mix until just smooth. Gently fold in the jam and most of the crushed meringue.

Microwave for 1 minute 10 seconds, or until risen and springy to the touch. Set aside to cool for 10 minutes.

For the topping, whip a few tablespoons of cream in a bowl until it forms soft peaks. Spoon the whipped cream over the cooled cake, then add a few strawberries and sprinkle with the remaining crushed meringue.

Dig in.

FRUITY

Lemon and poppy seed

2 tablespoons sunflower oil

3 tablespoons plus 1 teaspoon caster (superfine) sugar

1 medium egg

zest and juice of 1 lemon

4 tablespoons self-raising (self-rising) flour

1 tablespoon poppy seeds

In your mug, mix together the oil, 3 tablespoons of sugar, and the egg and lemon zest using a fork until smooth. Add the flour and poppy seeds, and mix until just smooth.

Microwave for 1 minute 20 seconds, or until risen and springy to the touch. Set aside to cool while you make the drizzle.

Meanwhile, mix 1 tablespoon of the lemon juice with the remaining 1 teaspoon of sugar to make a drizzle. Prick the cake using a fork and pour over the drizzle. Leave for 10 minutes for the cake to soak up the drizzle, then dig in and enjoy.

FRUITY

Makes
1

Ready in
5
minutes

Bakewell

2 tablespoons raspberry jam

2 tablespoons sunflower oil

3 tablespoons soft light brown sugar

1 medium egg

½ teaspoon almond extract

4 tablespoons self-raising (self-rising) flour

1 heaped tablespoon ground almonds

1 heaped teaspoon flaked (slivered) almonds

icing (confectioner's) sugar, to decorate

Evenly spread 1 tablespoon of the jam in the bottom of your mug. In a small bowl, mix together the oil, sugar, egg and almond extract using a fork until smooth. Add the flour and ground almonds, and mix until just smooth. Pour the batter into your mug. Add the remaining tablespoon of jam and gently swirl it in. Sprinkle over the flaked almonds.

Microwave for 1 minute 10 seconds, or until risen and springy to the touch. Dust with icing sugar and enjoy.

Orange and almond

2 tablespoons sunflower oil

3 tablespoons caster (superfine) sugar

1 medium egg

zest of 1 small orange

4 tablespoons ground almonds

scant ½ teaspoon baking powder

In your mug, mix together the oil, sugar, egg and orange zest using a fork until smooth. Add the ground almonds and baking powder, and mix until just smooth.

Microwave for 1 minute 20 seconds, or until risen and springy to the touch, and enjoy.

Festive fun

Ready in

4

minutes

Birthday sprinkles

2 tablespoons sunflower oil

3 tablespoons caster (superfine) sugar

1 medium egg

½ teaspoon vanilla extract

4 tablespoons self-raising (self-rising) flour

1 tablespoon sprinkles (I used Funfetti), plus extra to decorate

2 tablespoons ready-made buttercream icing, to decorate

In your mug, mix together the oil, sugar, egg and vanilla using a fork until smooth. Add the flour and mix until just smooth. Stir in the sprinkles.

Microwave for 1 minute 10 seconds, or until risen and springy to the touch. Set aside to cool for 10 minutes.

Once cool, either dollop or pipe on the buttercream icing. Scatter over a few more sprinkles and dig in.

Tip:

To make your own buttercream, beat 1 tablespoon softened salted butter with 4 tablespoons icing (confectioner's) sugar, a few drops of vanilla extract, ½ teaspoon milk of your choice, and a couple of drops of food colouring of your choice.

FESTIVE FUN

Gingerbread

2 tablespoons sunflower oil

3 tablespoons dark muscovado sugar

1 medium egg

1 tablespoon golden (light corn) syrup

1 teaspoon ground ginger

½ teaspoon mixed spice

4 tablespoons self-raising (self-rising) flour

2–3 mini gingerbread people or ½ large gingerbread person, broken into small pieces

1 tablespoon icing (confectioner's) sugar and a few small sweets (I used Jelly Tots), to decorate

In your mug, mix together the oil, sugar, egg and syrup using a fork until smooth. Add the ginger, mixed spice and flour, and mix until just smooth. Gently stir the pieces of gingerbread into the top half of the batter.

Microwave for 1 minute 10 seconds, or until risen and springy to the touch. Set aside to cool for about 10 minutes.

Make the icing, mix the icing sugar with ½ teaspoon of water in a small bowl. Drizzle it over the cake, top with a few small sweets, then dig in and enjoy.

Ready in
8
minutes

Hot chocolate with marshmallows

2 tablespoons sunflower oil

2 tablespoons caster (superfine) sugar

1 medium egg

1 teaspoon vanilla extract

3 tablespoons self-raising (self-rising) flour

1 tablespoon hot chocolate powder

1 heaped tablespoon mini or 3 regular marshmallows

In your mug, mix together the oil, sugar, egg and vanilla using a fork until smooth. Add the flour and hot chocolate powder, and mix until just smooth.

Microwave for 1 minute 10 seconds, or until risen and springy to the touch.

Scatter over the marshmallows, then microwave for a further 10 seconds. Allow a couple of minutes for the marshmallows to cool, then dig in and enjoy.

FESTIVE FUN

Makes
1

Ready in
4
minutes

Candy cane and white chocolate crunch

1 candy cane

2 tablespoons sunflower oil

3 tablespoons caster (superfine) sugar

1 medium egg

½ teaspoon vanilla extract

4 tablespoons self-raising (self-rising) flour

1 tablespoon white chocolate chips or chunks

vanilla ice cream, to serve

Before you begin, smash up the candy cane in a small bowl using the bottom of a rolling pin, then set aside.

In your mug, mix together the oil, sugar, egg and vanilla using a fork until smooth. Add the flour and mix until just smooth. Gently fold the crushed candy cane and white chocolate into to the top half of the batter.

Microwave for 1 minute 20 seconds, or until risen and springy to the touch. Sprinkle with any remaining candy cane dust and enjoy with a scoop of vanilla ice cream.

FESTIVE FUN

Ready in
5
minutes

Chocolate eggs

2 tablespoons sunflower oil

3 tablespoons golden caster (superfine) sugar

1 medium egg

½ teaspoon vanilla extract

4 tablespoons self-raising (self-rising) flour

4 candy-covered chocolate mini eggs, roughly chopped into quarters, plus 3 to decorate

In your mug, mix together the oil, sugar, egg and vanilla using a fork until smooth. Add the flour and mix until just smooth. Gently fold the chocolate egg pieces into the top half of the batter.

Microwave for 1 minute 20 seconds, or until risen and springy to the touch.

Finish by sprinkling over more chopped mini eggs and enjoy.

FESTIVE FUN

The shamrock

2 tablespoons sunflower oil

3 tablespoons caster (superfine) sugar

1 medium egg

½ teaspoon vanilla extract

¼ teaspoon peppermint extract

a few drops of green food colouring

4 tablespoons self-raising (self-rising) flour

3 tablespoons ready-made buttercream icing, to decorate

a maraschino cherry, to decorate

In your mug, mix together the oil, sugar, egg, vanilla and peppermint extracts and the green food colouring using a fork until smooth. Add the flour and mix until just smooth.

Microwave for 1 minute 10 seconds, or until risen and springy to the touch. Leave to cool for about 10 minutes, then dollop or pipe on the buttercream icing. Top with the cherry, then dig in and enjoy.

Tip:
To make your own buttercream, beat 1 tablespoon softened salted butter with 4 tablespoons icing (confectioner's) sugar, a few drops of vanilla extract, ½ teaspoon milk of your choice, and a couple of drops of food colouring of your choice.

Happy hour

Makes
1

Ready in
4
minutes

Rum raisin

2 tablespoons sunflower oil

3 tablespoons golden caster (superfine) sugar

1 medium egg

1 ½ tablespoons dark rum

4 tablespoons self-raising (self-rising) flour

1 tablespoon raisins

FOR THE GLAZE

1 teaspoon butter, melted

1 teaspoon rum

2 tablespoons icing (confectioner's) sugar

In your mug, mix together the oil, sugar, egg and rum using a fork until smooth. Add the flour and mix until smooth. Drop in the raisins one by one, trying to distribute them around the batter, but do not stir in.

Microwave for 1 minute 20 seconds, or until risen and springy to the touch. Set aside to cool for about 10 minutes while you make your glaze.

For the glaze, mix the butter with the rum and icing sugar in a small bowl. Spread over your cooled cake, then dig in and enjoy.

Makes
1

Ready in
4
minutes

Old fashioned

4 tablespoons plain
(all-purpose) flour

½ teaspoon baking powder

3 tablespoons soft light brown
sugar

2 tablespoons sunflower oil

1 medium egg

2 tablespoons bourbon

2 shakes of angostura bitters

zest of ½ orange

vanilla ice cream or double
(pouring) cream, to serve

In your mug, mix together the flour, baking powder
and sugar using a fork until combined. Add the oil,
egg, bourbon, bitters and orange zest, and mix
until just smooth.

Microwave for 1 minute 20 seconds, or until risen
and springy to the touch. Top with a scoop of ice
cream, then dig in and enjoy.

Makes
1

Ready in
5
minutes

Espresso martini

2 tablespoons soft light brown sugar

2 tablespoons plain (all-purpose) flour

1 tablespoon cocoa (unsweetened chocolate) powder

¼ teaspoon baking powder

1 medium egg

2 tablespoons sunflower oil

1 tablespoon espresso or double-strength coffee, cooled to room temperature

1 tablespoon coffee-flavoured liqueur (I used Kahlua)

1 tablespoon vodka

mascarpone, to serve

In your mug, mix together the sugar, flour, cocoa and baking powder with a fork until combined. Add the egg, oil, coffee, coffee liqueur and vodka, and mix until just smooth.

Microwave for 1 minute 20 seconds, or until risen and springy to the touch. This cake has a big rise in the microwave, but then sinks to become gorgeous and fudgy. Serve with a dollop of mascarpone and enjoy.

Makes
1

Ready in
4
minutes

Spiced rum and banana

1 small very ripe banana

2 tablespoons sunflower oil

3 tablespoons golden caster (superfine) sugar

1 medium egg

1 tablespoon spiced rum (I used Sailor Jerry), plus extra to serve

¼ teaspoon mixed spice

4 tablespoons self-raising (self-rising) flour

⅛ teaspoon baking powder

vanilla ice cream, to serve

In your mug, mash the banana and mix in the oil, sugar, egg, spiced rum using a fork until fully combined. Add the mixed spice, flour and baking powder, and mix until just smooth.

Microwave for 1 minute 20 seconds, or until risen and springy to the touch. Top with a scoop of ice cream, followed by a spoonful of rum, then dig in.

Amaretto
and chocolate

3 tablespoons self-raising
(self-rising) flour

1 tablespoon cocoa
(unsweetened chocolate)
powder

3 tablespoons soft light brown
sugar

1 tablespoon ground almonds

2 tablespoons sunflower oil

1 medium egg

2 tablespoons amaretto
(I used Disaronno)

crushed amaretti biscuit, to
decorate

In your mug, mix together the flour, cocoa, sugar
and ground almonds using a fork until combined.
Add the oil, egg and amaretto, and mix until just
smooth.

Microwave for 1 minute 10 seconds, or until risen
and springy to the touch. Top with the crushed
amaretti biscuit, then dig in and enjoy.

Irish cream cheesecake

1 teaspoon butter, melted, plus extra for greasing

1 digestive biscuit (graham cracker), crushed

2 tablespoons icing (confectioner's) sugar

2 tablespoons sour cream

2 tablespoons full-fat soft cheese (I used Philadelphia)

1 medium egg

2 tablespoons Irish cream liqueur (I used Baileys)

cocoa (unsweetened chocolate) powder, to decorate

Grease the inside of your mug with a little butter.

In your mug, mix together the crushed biscuit and melted butter, then press down to make a base.

In a small bowl, mix the icing sugar with the sour cream, soft cheese, egg and Irish cream liqueur using a hand whisk. Pour the mixture into your mug.

Microwave for 40 seconds. Leave to rest for 5 seconds, then microwave for a further 10 seconds. Leave to rest for 5 seconds, then microwave for another 20 seconds. Chill the cheesecake in the refrigerator for at least 45 minutes. Dust with cocoa and dig in.

Index

Acknowledgements

Massive thanks to the team behind this book. Issy, for your support and guidance, Nikki, for your design, Valeria for your incredible assistance in the kitchen, Hannah for your flawless taste and mind-reading abilities and Clare, for bringing beauty to every shot! Thank you to my friends and family for always being at the ready to give me their honest opinion on flavour and texture, especially Bo, my chief taste-tester who would happily eat mug cakes everyday. Lastly, thank you to Eve, my fairy food-mother.

About the author

Kate Calder is a trained chef, writer, recipe tester and food stylist with more than a decade's worth of experience in the kitchens of *BBC GoodFood*, *Olive* and *Good Housekeeping* magazines. She's written and styled for many publications but equally enjoys testing other chefs' recipes at home and feeding her friends & neighbours. This is her second cookbook, she is also the author of *3 Ingredient Cocktails*. Hailing from Toronto Canada, but now based in London with her young family, Kate's passion for food led her away from her previous career in the film industry but she continues to watch an unhealthy amount of film and tv.